First World War
and Army of Occupation
War Diary
France, Belgium and Germany

41 DIVISION
Headquarters, Branches and Services
Royal Army Ordnance Corps
Deputy Assistant Director Ordnance Services
27 April 1916 - 31 October 1917

WO95/2624/3

The Naval & Military Press Ltd
www.nmarchive.com
Published in association with The National Archives

Published by

The Naval & Military Press Ltd

Unit 10 Ridgewood Industrial Park,

Uckfield, East Sussex,

TN22 5QE England

Tel: +44 (0) 1825 749494

www.naval-military-press.com

www.nmarchive.com

This diary has been reprinted in facsimile from the original. Any imperfections are inevitably reproduced and the quality may fall short of modern type and cartographic standards.

© **Crown Copyright**
Images reproduced by permission of The National Archives, London, England, 2015.

Contents

Document type	Place/Title	Date From	Date To
Heading	WO95/2624/3		
Heading	D.A.D. Ord. Serv. May 1916-1917 Oct Mar 1918-Nov 1919		
War Diary	Boulogne	27/04/1916	27/04/1916
War Diary	Bailleul	28/04/1916	28/04/1916
War Diary	Merris	29/04/1916	29/05/1916
War Diary	Steenwerck	30/05/1916	16/08/1916
War Diary	Fletre	17/08/1916	21/08/1916
War Diary	Amiens	22/08/1916	23/08/1916
War Diary	Ailly-Le Haut-Clocher	24/08/1916	05/09/1916
War Diary	Buire Sur Ancre	06/09/1916	10/09/1916
War Diary	Belle Vue Farm Near Albert	11/09/1916	30/09/1916
War Diary	Albert (near)	01/10/1916	16/10/1916
War Diary	Hallencourt	17/10/1916	19/10/1916
War Diary	Fletre	20/10/1916	23/10/1916
War Diary	Reninghelst	24/10/1916	28/02/1917
Heading	War Diary of D.A. D.O.S. 41st Division For Month of March 1917		
War Diary	Reninghelst	01/03/1917	30/06/1917
War Diary	Berthen	01/07/1917	29/07/1917
War Diary	Westoutre	01/08/1917	14/08/1917
War Diary	Berthen	15/08/1917	20/08/1917
War Diary	Wizernes	21/08/1917	15/09/1917
War Diary	Zevecoten	15/09/1917	22/09/1917
War Diary	Caestre	23/09/1917	25/09/1917
War Diary	La Panne	26/09/1917	05/10/1917
War Diary	St. Idesbalde	07/10/1917	28/10/1917
War Diary	Malo Les Bains	29/10/1917	31/10/1917

Great [bam]

Great [bam]

41ST DIVISION

D. A. D. ORD. SERV.

MAY 1916 - ~~DEC~~ 1917 OCT

MAR 1918 — NOV 1919

LESS 1917 NOV } ITALY
1918 FEB

Army Form C. 2118

WAR DIARY
or
INTELLIGENCE SUMMARY
(Erase heading not required.)

41 R. DADoS.

Instructions regarding War Diaries and Intelligence Summaries are contained in F. S. Regs., Part II. and the Staff Manual respectively. Title Pages will be prepared in manuscript.

Place	Date	Hour	Summary of Events and Information	Remarks and references to Appendices
BOULOGNE	27/4/16		Crossed to Boulogne took Usual Sally	
BAILLEUL	28/4/16		Spoke to HQ II Corp Sec'd Army. ADS	
MERRIS	29/4/16		Visits various DDsMS - Field Dump	
	30/4/16		Reported to DDOS HQ Second Army	
	1/5/16		Returned after seen Entrenched Au'd Group	
	2/5/16		Visit to ADOS and to STEENWERCK (Padders)	
	3/5/16		Visit to ADOS of 1st Div.	
	4/5/16		Saw HQ travel	
	5/5/16		Spoke to DDMS	
	6/5/16		Commands Dumps Satisfactorily organised. Took Div prisoners	
	11/5/16		Visit for ADOS saw Advd TP, saw by lorry for Citeux	
	12/5/16		Saw Adv D.T.P. Saw Convoy & Saw Gen Bt. Mobile arrival of 4 Mobile Section	
	13/5/16		Saw DT Mobile supplies Div Horse	
	14/5/16		Visit ADOS	
			482 Saw Reports	
	15/5/16		Visit to ADOS saw him G Flaquine (12, 17) Div	
	16/5/16		Saw arrived Reports	

Army Form C. 2118

WAR DIARY
or
INTELLIGENCE SUMMARY
(Erase heading not required.)

Instructions regarding War Diaries and Intelligence Summaries are contained in F. S. Regs., Part II. and the Staff Manual respectively. Title Pages will be prepared in manuscript.

D.A.D.O.S. 41 Div W
Vol 1

Place	Date	Hour	Summary of Events and Information	Remarks and references to Appendices

[Handwritten war diary entries, largely illegible due to faded pencil writing. Entries dated from 17/5/16 through 31/5/16, referring to places MERRIS and Steenwerck, mentioning items including periscopes, signposts, visits to Brigade/Division HQ, Col. Cassel, messages, ballet, etc.]

WAR DIARY
or
INTELLIGENCE SUMMARY

Army Form C. 2118

DADOS June
41 Div
Vol 2

Place	Date	Hour	Summary of Events and Information	Remarks and references to Appendices
Steenwerck	June 1		None. No. 14 Envelopes altogether now issued	
	June 2		Nobody seems clear what units are Corps troops supplied by nor Divisional ADS	
	June 3		Mr Bryl Bde found glass of Rum No. 14 Envelope broken ? How. I am told that this may happen spontaneously & hurts nobody's feelings	
	June 4		Went to Dieppe & Bailleul	
	June 5		Had Saws the A — quite unfounded — delusions among units that to ask is a little for issue. This is shared by people who ought to know better	
	June 6		Visit from ADDS	
	June 7		Div. Schools to galore are created, but no provision for supplying any stores is made. The barrelings all come to me, & expect to be supplied with things which are not there & cannot be got unless authorised	
	June 8		I got the Evil Gas Officer to raise the issue at Bde. Confs as to Showbaths Glorious. It appears the very short of Rum and also of Horns — if he right there A3 as I believed	
	June 9		Went to see ADDS in his room at Bailleul — Ordered by 2nd Army to cancel my indent for Stokes Mortars which ADDS had told me to send	
	June 10		Still no real settlement of our Ihmch stew question. It was undoubtedly "done down" by A. Burson, but steps to remedy are hopefully in hand	
	June 11		Took & got some Vermorel Sprayers at II Corps Workshops	
	June 12		The ADDS Misses brings a welcome letter in correspondence from the Corps. Saw ADDS who is going to Hospital. Suffers, poor J am sorry for the last long. Caused to feel a bit as he is now fraysally	

WAR DIARY
or
INTELLIGENCE SUMMARY
(Erase heading not required.)

Army Form C. 2118

Place	Date	Hour	Summary of Events and Information	Remarks and references to Appendices
Steenwerck	June 13		Had a visit from ADOS & Corps via my ADMS. He was able to give me or two pieces of useful information	
	June 14		Blankets coming in from units in enough weather. Hope that Spontaneous Combustion will not result	
	June 15		Day adjourned the some let right - Went to Estaires & got samples of British Covers	
	June 16		Went to Bailleul for local prices of caps	
	June 17		Blankets being returned - weather heavenly. It was decided to have Covers & not British Covers. Must letter (brother stiff) regulate myself	
	June 18		Estaires, Merville & finally Hazebrouck to get Caps - wanted 1200 yds - all shops hopeless, led to pay absurd price but no choice	
	June 19		up to quantity one day. Went to HQ XIRB 1 Bo.	
			To Bailleul & Estaires. Saw DADOS 2d Div? re getting leg protectors v. barbed wire. Agreed to buy 1000 Bruch Covers	
	June 20		Div? passed to X Corps via II Corps	
	June 21		Went to Bailleul, Hazebrouck, Merville, Estaires, trying to get protectors leggings	
	June 22		Nothing to note	
	June 23		Machine gun parts - cylinders & return springs - Cavalry anxiously as none attainable	
	June 24		ADOS Came in morning. To Bailleul in afternoon	
			To Estaires & bought 1000 set of 4000 Rifle Covers. Trouble with 15 Echelon SAC who seem to have none of their stores	
			from the late SAC	
	June 25		48 Bil Sgts for 18 pr Battries arrived	
	June 26		To Estaires in morning, trying first Elastic Laces. Got some at Hazebrouck in afternoon, but too bad a lot of getting	
	June 27		Nothing beyond office. A day out rising a midnight trip to officers' fund	
	June 28		To Estaires, bought but more Rifle Covers. Visited N2 1 B in Hospital in afternoon. ADOS Came stile I was out	
	June 29		Horses bought 1000 Rifle Covers got 4000 from Base of British Covers, but have not been unduly precipitate	
	June 30		The ADMS gave supplies still a constant anxiety. If horses abroad	

J. Spongen Cpt
ADMS 6+ Dw+
30 WD

41 July
Army Form C. 2118
DADOS
41 D.D. Vol 3

WAR DIARY [July 1916]
or
INTELLIGENCE SUMMARY Sheet 1
(Erase heading not required.)

Place	Date	Hour	Summary of Events and Information	Remarks and references to Appendices
STEENBECQUE	July 1		[illegible handwritten entries for July 1–23, 1916]	

WAR DIARY or INTELLIGENCE SUMMARY (Sheet 2)

Army Form C. 2118

Place	Date	Hour	Summary of Events and Information	Remarks and references to Appendices
STEENWERCK	July 24		A.D.S.S. Came	
	July 25		To Bailleul for kilts 2nd Dragoons & Flieder Jackes	
	July 26		Nothing to note	
	July 27		A.D.S.S. Came. Saw H.Q. as to lewis magazine carriers being taken away & put up a letter about it	
	July 28		Went to Estaires & Flagstaff with a view given inventors for munitions	
	July 29		1000 Steel Helmets arrived	
	July 30		Had to issue to 2nd Army as to 18 Pr. R.O. Springs in view of shortage	
	July 31		A.D.S.S. Came. Went to H.Q. 2nd I.B.	

J Sharpe Capt
D.A.D.O.S. 4 Div

31/7/1916

Vol 4 Aug
Army Form C. 2118

WAR DIARY August 1916
or
INTELLIGENCE SUMMARY (Sheet 1)
(Erase heading not required.)

PADOS 41 Div
PADOS

Place	Date 1916	Hour	Summary of Events and Information	Remarks and references to Appendices
STEENWERCK	Aug 1st		Weekly DMS meeting. Discussed question of undertaking in event of move. They only forward full scale of beds. Very desirable	
	Aug 2nd		Received 8 Travoys No. 5 in place of No. 14. Went to Corps Siding at Bailleul	
	Aug 3rd		ADMS looked at some lost shoes, as Greyhounds have been used as to No. 3 tin tins	
	Aug 4th		Visited 9th to 113 Bde M.G. Coy	
	Aug 5th		ADMS Came.	
	Aug 6th		Went to Mr des Cats Supply School - also to see ADMS 35 Div to glean information as to working in the Somme district	
	Aug 7th		Went to Claes Black - Col Grigson and me all day depot shops. The work is astounding most interesting & busily organised	
	Aug 8th		Went to 8th Division Bailleul & Col B.S. Meds conveyances as to issue of undesirable	
	Aug 9th		Brought HQ. Horsery Wagons at Bailleul	
	Aug 10th		Met Major Jackson to discuss G.O.C. played as to 18 pr Turning out Spong. O'Vere appointed A.K.O. actor	
	Aug 11th		ADMS Came in morning. Went to Bailleul - DDMS came in afternoon. 12,000 Socks arrived at Corps?	
	Aug 12th		Col Coleman came to view	
	Aug 13th		Stress beyond the Balanced. Lunch work do not wait to move on convoy transport. 49 New Carts Came	
	Aug 14th		Went to Bail B.S. to Corps Q as to better in our new area	
	Aug 15th		Went to Nellis & Bailleul to Bail.U.S. Yellow Trigrads not yet ready - now promised for Tuesday. Have arranged to take over 23rd Div ADS Shop. ADMS 23rd Div Came Came in morning	

1875 Wt. W593/846 1,000,000 4/15 J.B.C. & A. A.D.S.S./Forms/C. 2118.

WAR DIARY or INTELLIGENCE SUMMARY

August 1916 (Sheet 2)

Army Form C. 2118

Place	Date	Hour	Summary of Events and Information	Remarks and references to Appendices
STEENWERCK	Aug 16	A	ADMS 23 Div. Came for ride arrangements about transfer. Went to P.A.M. Nuppé. Rules as to undertaking &c.	
	Aug 17	A	Moved to Hellu. Took over premises occupied by the 23rd Div. Advance Who charged about with us	
	Aug 18	A	Wired that no stores to taken from Clees after Monday. 2nd Army ordered that. Have be told them early to tell for Gen: Woed to Blaisie started	
	Aug 19	A	No clothing came up from Base. Units drawing about drawing kit we have. 23rd Div. DADOS fetched to local places	
	Aug 20	A	19 two gun cats & large amount of stores (including clothing). Hope that units will clear their stores away before we move	
			Many of the tent beds for 23 Div. broke on trollies.	
	Aug 21	A	To Steenie to get Sisters still canvas. Arranged with RTO Cook to have to trucks for our move	
AMIENS	Aug 22	"	To Amiens by Car with AA & QMG and ADVS. Stayed there.	
	Aug 23	"	Went round with Div. Area to all Bde HQ.	
AILLY-LE HAUT-CROCHER	Aug 24	"	Left Amiens for Ailly. 11 O'clock. Visited Supply Col en route & arranged as to 4 ADS lorries	
	Aug 25	A	Went to Vignacourt. Stores to be filled on the company to move. Arranged to stick Gnos blankets &c.	
	Aug 26	A	Went to Amiens to HQ XV Corps. Brought American cots for hospitals signalling. 26 new gnos = 8 to late 1½ better.	
	Aug 27	A	To Port Remy about 4 1814 and 1 4.5 not landed over by 23rd Div. Went with RA Sfty Capt to ADoS & Corps & to Havupt with him to ADS holdup. ADoS informed me in afternoon that GnosMed RA to put them. Went to HQ on day Lest in by 11th Division on the day & gradually stayed still	
	Aug 28	A	Leave gnos stores Cecil a good deal of anxiety. Reported to HQ on day.	
	Aug 29	A	No 9 Princeps was beginning to get supplied up to extract a large number Cairns to day	
	Aug 30	"	Types of new tents Carts all going very steady on round at type.	
	Aug 31	"	Went to CRA as to Princeps, new newly complete for RAM & to HQ XV Corps. Mixed ADoS idle Ca.m. here.	J. Sprangs Capt. DADoS 4.1 Div. 31/8/16

41. Army Form C. 2118
Vol 5
Sept 1916

WAR DIARY
INTELLIGENCE SUMMARY (Sheet 1)
(Erase heading not required.)

Place	Date	Hour	Summary of Events and Information	Remarks and references to Appendices
AILLY L	Sept	1	Artillery ordered to move to-day. Wind him to Belgium. No 5 Presque of divns 4 to 10.14. No reply. Duty bien trophically of the move	
A Clochers	Sept	2	No conveyance appear to have been made for Sunday stores to the R.A. who are 25 mls off. Wired for gas & ammo for C.183 Bde.	
	Sept	3	No stores came up. Wired C.R.A. proposing to send lorry with stores then. – Asked Q as to reserve gas details now at VIGNACOURT	
	Sept	4	Sent lorry to R.A. 35 road miles off with stores. Have wired 1000 Steel Wrists in last 2 days. Told Q 5 lorries will be wanted for	
	Sept	5	Preparation for moving. Conv written to Q. and others — a long journey. Wrote to ADOS as to heavy traveling or bulking gun-lay stores	
BURE Sur	Sept	6	Moved to BURE. Bump ready on old marquee at S. of road. Fortunately sooner to find, as little in way of report here	
	Sept	7	Went to ADOS XV Corps and to PERICOURT – trying to find my kestrel	
	Sept	8	Huge amount of stores ordering from here pats to break takes care to ALBERT. Am thankful we do keep from lost stores at	
			Proposed to know to VIGNACOURT for R.M. Units Units from Havre to detail (1st still) demands for Box dispensers. Ordination is done	
			Havre always seems to resists	
	Sept	9	Went to 55 R.A. Stay to inspect our probable new bump, which is in open ground. Hope to get stores lot from Corps that will	
			be read. Wired for more steel Wounds	
	Sept	10	Cannot find out whether 7" or 9" R.A. have been moved to us. As 7" Ordnance say Ordnls coming in from tim	
Belle Vue	Sept	11	Moved up to day. believing 55" Division & locating troubles where they were	
Farm near	Sept	12	82 large cots (weighing over 16) arrived, indent days open — went to Amiens in afternoon to make purchase	
ALBERT	Sept	13	Wired for days supplies – Every steel Wounds have now come to Equip to scale but new drafts are frequently arriving	
	Sept	14	To Amiens in morning, got a lot of adult tops. New tentage arrives. Sten cost to the catchers	
	Sept	15	Advance begins. Div took Flers. 3 Guns for 7" Bow R.A. (1 opbs)	
	Sept	16	Selected H 9.45 JMs from Pluteust, which R.A. do not want & can't move, but we have to take them & let them be idle.	

WAR DIARY Sept. 1916 (Sheet 2)
or
INTELLIGENCE SUMMARY
(Erase heading not required.)

Army Form C. 2118

Place	Date	Hour	Summary of Events and Information	Remarks and references to Appendices
	Sept. 17		"Div" moves to RIBEMONT to-morrow. Sit at RA & 125 I.B. terrain up line. Am not going to migrate but leave my Rear Stuff	
	Sept. 18		A pouring day - roads flooded for hours. RIBEMONT is now my Gallant unfortunately	
	Sept. 19		Went to Div HQ at RIBEMONT and to A.DoS 15 Corps, who was not. Returned an hr pk, with B.M. to A.D.S. lickings as it opened late	
	Sept. 20		Saw the 7th Div - did not impect it. Refilling points bring in large Reserve gun elements, but some tents have long nothing to time & little time to spare	
	Sept. 21		Got round big liveries to report stores mostly. Rain then. & notes Complaints.	
	Sept. 22		20 kind guns to right. The three 4 to come. State DM & Wishes to come. Went to Ovens for police in afternoon	
	Sept. 23		18 pdrs for 5/189 & A/149 have arrived at Brilliant. 2 Vickers guns for 122 J.B. Got Expect Woolf & Stores Inn pulls of Subery dump	
	Sept. 24		ADoS came & money. Went to him in afternoon too HQ & 1 Corps H.Q. Heavy Pde. Wishings ahead but light learners have we got	
	Sept. 25		all line guns. Vickers & DMGs - Vickers doing to right. Large amount of stores trickling much wanted less Magazines came to right. Arranged with "D" to have waggons up to S/B of demand as trails look so very dirty the last attack	
	Sept. 26		Many GS, Mess, Anan Vickers galore. Started by Shells - 7th RA constantly wanting new guns	
	Sept. 27		Stores have come up in large quantities lately. Hope "Div" will be fairly refitted as to essentials	
	Sept. 28		Hear Casualty 7th RA are going Lots of harpons & 2 guns (not carriage) awaiting him. Hope they will collect	letters Annoyed
	Sept. 29		Went to Div HQ - 55th Div went off. So we had no way of sending telegrams to Div HQ - send through them. "Bulk" come to Rouen apparently never reported by 55th last night	
	Sept. 30		Marched to Guardy. Return of Bulk for 3 weeks prepared. Find it difficult to Commissaries with B.H.Q. under present circumstances. Telephones not Connected	

Army Form C. 2118

RADD's
October 1916
41 Div Vol 6
1st Part

WAR DIARY
or
INTELLIGENCE SUMMARY
(Erase heading not required.)

Instructions regarding War Diaries and Intelligence Summaries are contained in F.S. Regs., Part II. and the Staff Manual respectively. Title Pages will be prepared in manuscript.

Place	Date	Hour	Summary of Events and Information	Remarks and references to Appendices
ALBERT (near)	Oct 1		Went to DHQ to see GOC as to Jarters. Also to 124 TB. Anow took out two eggs on Wagons are standard t30 Arrowhead	
	Oct 2		To AMIENS. purchasing. 21st Bn RA moved to me. Journied Rain	
	Oct 3		Mud everywhere. Lorries very important. Unloading stores a "nightmare" - Everything soaked to ground	
	Oct 4		Stores accumulating as units can't transport. Deluge of calls for reports on the tests the sites for workshops (ie) to be Corps. Units are at present engaged in more vital business than replying to these Commandments, so I can't get any suitable theses	
	Oct 5		Got candid opinion on question of challenging articles on vehicles (Quite 3 guns worth if a solid led record it)	
	Oct 6		Great scarcity of Tiffits. Explosive the point of few JS second judicial data on ADS business matters	Max Zoom
	Oct 7		Start worries of vehicles to to a man to Cavallation - a log to Unsatisfactory bit - Water bottles to ground. deputy	
	Oct 8		Pat of OHQ. On run on to Quarry close by bit. Q at FRICOURT. Luckily got 12" Siv" to correct my telephone	sed hibmets to Got stuck x did not return
	Oct 9		Transport question will soon become acute, Units being in bad of things, accentuates it. My long tour to did out	
	Oct 10		Managed to get a lot of things - utility stal hibmets - for Salvage Several demands for lost or destroyed Lewis guns come in	
	Oct 11		Went the BHQ who move to morrow	
	Oct 12		BHQ went back to BUSSE on units coming into rest. Hors odd. Thight boots arrived Stir is now v. Crystal	Complete with spare parts bag
	Oct 13		11 Lewis guns came up. Had asked Brigades to make to Morris & Maskart Wards for spare of Lewis guns. These guns are	
	Oct 14		9 new Lewis guns drawn as to reserve.	
	Oct 15		Units as to many stores are exhausted appear to have been made. 29 M Siv" took to busy TMS asking Reces So not know how to deal with to days enemy stores	
	Oct 16		Lorries full went to ASGUILLON. ATC signed to order them as first loads	
HAILLENCOURT	Oct 17		Managed to get loads at MEAULCOURT & hope but they will get through all right. Had to Transport enemy stores without unloading Printed to HALLENCOURT on 2 Corps order. Lorries got in very late but stores would be rated Wind Reconnaissance v ABBEVILLE & telephoned VIGNACOURT to send all stores straight to II Army without Halting	

1875 Wt. W593/826 1,000,000 4/15 J.B.C. & A. A.D.S.S./Forms/C. 2118.

Army Form C. 2118

WAR DIARY
or
INTELLIGENCE SUMMARY
(Erase heading not required.)

October 1916
[2nd Sheet]

Instructions regarding War Diaries and Intelligence Summaries are contained in F. S. Regs., Part II. and the Staff Manual respectively. Title Pages will be prepared in manuscript.

Place	Date	Hour	Summary of Events and Information	Remarks and references to Appendices
HALLENCOURT	Oct.	18	Wind Calais to find stores on 21st	
	Oct.	19	Left HALLENCOURT. Wind for 15,000 blankets	
FLIXECOURT	Oct.	20	Bed to old Camp & Office at FLIXECOURT	
	Oct.	21	Went to RENINGHELST. Prepd Camp & tentstore. Wired for Second blanket order 15,000	
	Oct.	22	5350 blankets arrived & letter tombless drawn by units	To II Army in afternoon. Urgent
	Oct.	23	Gas Helmet Scare. Lorry sent to Cnams for 4000. This is orwy to trobs for Somme not yet arrvg. 900 Blankets received	
RENINGHELST	Oct.	24	Moved to RENINGHELST. Enormous quantity of stores including Small Box Respirators	
	Oct.	25	Blanket Respirators still coming. Stores asked Closs & Exps Cams & Coss, 1st Anzac.	
	Oct.	26	Pair of stores from Somme arrived ard a gun 18 pdr. Iwird to Home as it the, as it is a myty	
	Oct.	27	QM Mistry. Letters for Somme being distributed	
	Oct.	28	Blankets still coming in. Box respirators going out fast.	
	Oct.	29	Rinder of Somme stores arrived. Have tried to return gun. 4000 W.P. Cyps Cams up - 900 Camp for Exps	
	Oct.	30	48 T.M. Carts now received. Heard Lt. R.A. on Convoy back. Wind to Calais as to their limits clothy	
	Oct.	31	Have orgs for non RA units arrived. Stores are thankfully congested & with LITTRA Cams	

T.J. Sparrow Capt
Broos H Sec

WAR DIARY or INTELLIGENCE SUMMARY

Army Form C. 2118

November 1916
Sheet 1

Vol 7

Stamp: A.D.D.S. 30 NOV 1916 41st Divn

(Erase heading not required.)

Instructions regarding War Diaries and Intelligence Summaries are contained in F.S. Regs., Part II. and the Staff Manual respectively. Title Pages will be prepared in manuscript.

Place	Date	Hour	Summary of Events and Information	Remarks and references to Appendices
Rouen	1 Nov		10,500 socks - Boot brushes & some kit for Bn	
	2 Nov		Received CB repairs & repair kit and Boot lasts — the last 10 of our stores	
	3 Nov		6 PM Artillery Store very full and apparently no hope for Complaints	
	4 Nov		The number of clothing — demanding clothes because	
	5 Nov		20 Nov gave (— total of 16 pr. letter to all) used	
	6 Nov		R.A. wrote me to say will supply large amount of blankets & clothes as well as repairs	
	7 Nov		Store very full up to B.A. advises of detail stores blankets repairs to	
	8 Nov		arms came. Have had RA still not drawn for a day or two yet. Have accumulated the Complains	
	9 Nov		Went on leave	
	10 Nov		Got back 6.30 am today — Stores still to full	
	21 Nov		Reed. to Col. Secretary 8 168/7 supply list R.T. biddings not yet reed. O stows when demand Counter signed by O.O.S Formation	
	22 Nov		R.T. lorries arrived. Stored Kitchen P/G cylinder & 15 Mark V base	
	23 Nov		As DADGS received quarter of 4 socks per man. Would want Army Service	
	24 Nov		2 Handles for RA arrived. Stores nearly all issued at once. Meeting of BMS today	
	25 Nov		Brigade training at Brussels	
	26 Nov		Saw R.A. & to be in connection of Two Brigade tents 2 G Gun Artly Bde. Settled to cancel all ten front orders	
	27 Nov		Orders of gun bolts rept. 4 Lewis Patterns — 20 Cabs for R.T. bitships	
	28 Nov		Have demanded 18pdr guns — to fact that has been heard of any type	
	29 Nov		Under our Stores. But apparent will only be 2 weeks open which the a result nearly equal today as lately	
	30 Nov			

J Sparger Capt
BAOS 41 Div

WAR DIARY or INTELLIGENCE SUMMARY

Army Form C. 2118

DADOS 41st Div. December 1916 Vol 8

Stamp: D.A.D.O.S. 41st DIVISION 2 JAN 1917

Place	Date	Hour	Summary of Events and Information	Remarks and references to Appendices
RENINGHELST	Dec 2		Went to Army HQ as to provision of fowls for troops to roast Christmas	
	Dec 4		18 pdr gun arrived. I believe that Smith R.A is organiser - it to Corps, indirectly re staffing area. Went to ESTAIRES	
	Dec 6		v BAILLEUL. We could not get any suitable wendy fowls	
			Saw ADOS, the troops sent as sample for Calais	
	Dec 8		Went to X Corps at ABEELE. Pachydite Capes being altered - to be issued to Battalions	
	Dec 9		Went to BAILLEUL	
	Dec 10		Conference with A.D.O.S. + D.A.D.O.S. of other Div. at X Corps	
	Dec 12		Snow. Went to BAILLEUL for night shirts for patients	
	Dec 13		ADOS came in afternoon. Lt was at ADOS Camp	
	Dec 15		QM Meeting in morning. ADOS came	
	Dec 17		All battalions now have 12 Lewis guns - 2 men each having Carr - Except Pioneers (8)	
			The Signals seem to be insufficient in number + fresh Envoy not got in abnormally	
	Dec 19		GOC Enquiry as to clipping machines	large troops
	Dec 22		Meeting of QMs	
	Dec 23		ADOS came	
	Dec 25		Repairs (running) for 3" Stable now promised by them after being urged by ADOS. Bass say that none were due or indent	
	Dec 27		All the "belt" arrangements are to be changed for Tommy. Stores will only come on alternate days + Lays for ordering will be changed the weekly circularising all Bn Wounds. Have decided that stores cannot be issued under the new regime	
			Until the day following this arrival, at all corps in this short days when light only lasts up to 3 or 4 pm	
	Dec 28		New Stable DR for No 1 JPLB Went to BAILLEUL + ABEELE	
	Dec 29		Q.M. Meeting ADOS Came	

31/12/16

J Spurgin Capt
DADOS 41 Div

Army Form C. 2118

WAR DIARY
or
INTELLIGENCE SUMMARY
(Erase heading not required.)

SADS
4/ Div
January 1917

Vol 9

Instructions regarding War Diaries and Intelligence Summaries are contained in F.S. Regs, Part II. and the Staff Manual respectively. Title Pages will be prepared in manuscript.

Place	Date 1917	Hour	Summary of Events and Information	Remarks and references to Appendices
REDINGHURST	Jan 2		Lewis guns (riding 3) for instruction, issued to 122nd T.M. School	
	Jan 5		Q.M. Meeting —	
			Several slippers came - which were much wanted. No tools etc for Box. Went to ABEELE in afternoon	
	Jan 8		Just Lewis guns blown up for a day time. Intended the afternoon	
	Jan 9		Capt Lewis came up the morning. Wind for Vickers gun	
	Jan 10		Vickers of QM's White Carrom for show to Central guns very bright for us by 23rd Div?	
	Jan 12		Vickers gun for 123 M.G. Coy. Went to Bn HdQrs for trench shelters for horses. Any proposals against rain	
	Jan 13		12 No 75 Rugers came up. Also 8 Dural Scroll bags	
	Jan 14		Regants approved. Many wants QMs boiler suit for all Sigs to protective. This is constantly fatally	
	Jan 15		R.A. agree not sheets as not big enough. Meeting at Corps as to disposing stores at Railhead & stopping traffic after a bad frost	
	Jan 17		Q.M. Meeting. Units report that Infantry duffle are coming with web and not 1914 Equipment	
	Jan 19		Sent to be quartered at x Corps H.Q. by Gnl. Lawson as to C.O.C personnel. Gas Sgt Cornbrug out will render a lot of future turned	
	Jan 21		to Lepsy burrow but it can't be helped. Pitched star tent at Railhead in readiness for thaw.	
	Jan 22		Have got Trunks line. Eliminated Army will send team down that frost still continues	
	Jan 23		Went to BAILLEUL	
	Jan 25		Lt ERWIN arrived last night to look up duty & will take my place during absence on leave	
	26		Q.M. Meeting. Received a visit from ADDS	Absent on Private leave A.D.O.S 4th Divn a/c 19 Jan 1917 to 4th Jan 1917
	27		attended Branded Conference.	
	28		Capt Spranger went on leave	31 JAN 1917
	29		Went to Right land	
	30		18 Lah for A/187 Batty	

1875. Wt. W593/826 1,000,000 4/15. J.B.C. & A. A.D.S.S./Forms/C. 2118.

WAR DIARY or INTELLIGENCE SUMMARY

Army Form C. 2118.

(Erase heading not required.)

Instructions regarding War Diaries and Intelligence Summaries are contained in F.S. Regs., Part II. and the Staff Manual respectively. Title Pages will be prepared in manuscript.

UNITS: 41st Divn.
February 1917
Vol 10

Place	Date	Hour	Summary of Events and Information	Remarks and references to Appendices
RENINGHELST	1917 Feb			
	1	2-18	18 plat guns put out of action through fraternalism	
	2		Q.M meeting. 1 Leica gun for 2.3 Middlesex	
	3		Went to Bailleul	
	6		Went to Bailleul	
	7		Divisional Conference see the Engineer Reg'l Inclosure of 7.1.17 Batt out of action	
			A.D.O.S. called. M.A.P.S. 17th Divn.	
	9		Q.M meeting. 24 Lewis guns arrived	
	12		Went to Poperinghe	
	14		" Abeele, Bailleul + Steenwerck	
	16		Q.M meeting	
	18		1 Vickers gun put out of action	
	19		Went to Bailleul	
	23		Q.M meeting. 1 Lewis gun put out of action	
	26		A.D.O.S called. 21 rifles no damage recd from Base	
	27		Trans. relocation movement	
	24		1 Vickers & 1.18 pdr gun put out of action	
	28		Capt Spronger relieved from leave reported for Temp. Duty with ADOS I Corps.	

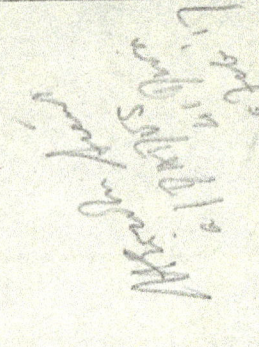

1 MAR 1917

~~Confidential~~

War Diary
of
D.A.D.O.S.
41st Division

For Month of March 1917

WAR DIARY
or
INTELLIGENCE SUMMARY

Army Form C. 2118.

D.A.D.O.S.
41st Div. March 1917

Place	Date	Hour	Summary of Events and Information	Remarks and references to Appendices
RENINGHELST	1917 March 1		Lewis gun destroyed by enemy fire	
	2		Div's Conference. Went to Bailleul	
	4		A.D.O.S. called	
	5		Demonstration of new "Rushcart" equipment before Div. Commander	
	7		Went to Abeele. Visited MGTS. 700 I Corps Troops. Drew 30 Horses Shoemakers	
	8		A.D.O.S. called. G.O.C. opened Divl Theatre	
	9		Divl Conference. Went to Bailleul	
	10		Recd German Brassard been captured by 10th R.W. Surrey Regt	
	12		Went to Cassel. Returned Divl Cyclists MO with reason shirt & 2nd Army	
	13		Went to Bailleul. A.D.S. arrived	
	16		Divl Conference	
	17		Visited a D.S. Went to Bailleul attended Conference HQ	
	19		Returned to Div. on ADOS Lorry back to x Corps HQ	
	23		Q.M. Conference. Blankets are to be issued via Hire Bags, which do not come from Base, in field	
	24		Divl Conference. Recd quotes of Boot repairs & Grenade Rifles	
	26		Sent MG Inf Bde Store for all Rlw units to STEENVOORDE by lorry & have arranged to continue this	
	27		Battn. now complete with 16 Lewis guns	
	29		ADOS Came	
	30		Q.M. Meeting. G.O.C. 113 I.B. called	
	31		Divl Conference. ADOS came.	

J Sparrow Capt.
DADOS 41 Div.
31/3/1917

Army Form C. 2118
[APRIL 1917]

WAR DIARY
or
INTELLIGENCE SUMMARY

(Erase heading not required.)

BAPOS
41st Div.

Place	Date	Hour	Summary of Events and Information	Remarks and references to Appendices
R FMNGHEAST	April 3 1917		Visit from D.O.S. who inspected Dumps etc. & ADOS & Corps.	
	April 6		Q.M's meeting. ADOS came. Visited 12.s Battery. 11th Mustard trippled stores	
	April 7		Div. Conference — Have arranged to send stores to Midivite for 122 Inf. Bde & 1st Fd. Bde. RFA	
	April 10		Saw Div. Comm'dr as to reduction of issues to troops & went through figures previously got out for his papers. Went to Banister on local points.	
	April 13		Q.M. Meeting. The Q.M.s recommend supply of Satchels for S.B. Respirators, as the satchels wear-out & whole respirator gets damaged etc.	
	April 14		Went to Banister re money — Div. Conference.	
	April 15		Sent C.R.A. particulars of issues of hard equipment to R.A.M units	
	April 17		B.G. 123 Inf. Bde called. Div. decided not to have Brand Clubs. Brd. Base Army stops to support. Had some het gun men to ride. Went to 125	
	April 18		B.G. 124 called. Hebrut (6 Brds.) came up — Good 'n all. In evening 47th Div. took them over Went to 123	
	April 19		Ride at Corpone in afternoon. ADOS called in morning	
	April 20		Q.M. Meeting — Went to Banister for telephone American Code	
	April 21		Div. Coga. Suggested let troops take their Hy. Cars instead of indenting for stores lying under their noses – so save time as well as money.	
	April 24		Saw A.D.O at Norbrut as to return of blankets etc. Went to HQ 122 I.B as to longing stores there keeping down	
	April 25		Went to BAPOS 23 & 39 Div. ADOS called	
	April 27		336 Was beg. issued, purchased by IDMSS 47th of course too got full supply from Base after that – C.O. meeting	
	April 28		Went to BAPOS 47th & 19 Div. Found C.O. & Ass-dept 23rd Middsx & Oxford all out – Div. Coga. Mentioned trouble	
	April 30		Boots & Socks & strict issue in each of men. Armies went to 122 Infde at ARGOUES	
	Oct		DMS Sy & DDI called	

1 MAY 19...

J Sharpe Capt.
30/4/17
D.A.D.O.S. of Div.

WAR DIARY or INTELLIGENCE SUMMARY

Army Form C. 2118.

BADOS
3rd Div.
4 Div."

May 1917

Vol 13

Place	Date 1917	Hour	Summary of Events and Information	Remarks and references to Appendices
REMINGHURST	May 2		Went to ABEELE. Saw ADOS as to getting tents & clothing away. Settled with dump at Prohart & Camp	
	3		Went to RCB as to getting kit arrangements fixed up	
	4		9 PM Conference. Went to 12a I.B. at ARCQUES	
	5		Div Conference	
	7		Find out Genl. units have been drawing stores last at SOMME & not stores demanded	
	9		Went to MERREBRUGGE & ARCQUES (HQ 12a & 13a Bn)	
	11		9 PM Conference	
	12		Out Conference. Went to see men near Balon Cos.	
	15		Went to HAZEBROUCK & BAILLEUL re johns list. Also arranged to try to mark duration after grenades. Not DB off 122 (B actual)	
	17		Saw QSC as to issue of stoves & gave him list	
	18		9 PM Meeting. Saw BADOS 24 Div. as to Canvas buys re Place of Pad Saddles for Convoys of ration	
	20		Went to BAILLEUR. Our van depriving of bags. Amount of Camp Stores & clothing of x Caps	
	21		Several problems of Grenades for Rifles — Convoys out to 123 I.B S.btel for trial & report as to best Stuff to adopt	
	22		ADOS called — A good deal of trouble of clothing etc has been sent away to Base	
	23		ADOS Arrd. called. Killing of stirrups Back Saddles (Bm sets) now issued	
	25		9 PM Meeting. Went to 2 Army RE Stops. My agent to have Grenade Canvas for RB Grenades made. But ill appear on 29th	
	26		ADOS called. Dur. Confce. Gun Park at GODSWAERSVELDE for all Div. Gun. Platoon MGs & Parks will appear on 29"	
	27		Filled dumps to Base will attack all Camp Stores less First Aid kits. Convoy to arrange before starting nearly disposed of	
	29		ADOS called. Started tailors in making Bakers bag seats Valise and Saddles for Convoy Colman	
			Gun Park opened at GODSWAERSVELDE. All Div. RA guns there. & 3 MGs of all kinds except 9.45, also all limen & MG Guns. Will come back	
	30		For Rev. ADOS called. Went to HQ 24 Div.	
	31		Received 12 2" TMs, bkells & bags. res. of late outfits Dodging stores for alluding by x Caps	
			Went to ABEELE. Saw ADOS	

J.F. Spragay Cap'n
BADOS 4 Div.
31/07/1917

WAR DIARY or INTELLIGENCE SUMMARY

Army Form C. 2118.

BASOS Sheet 1
41 Division
June 1917
Vol 14

Place	Date	Hour	Summary of Events and Information	Remarks and references to Appendices
KEMMELHOEK	June 1	1	QM Conference. Went to Brigade purchasing. 2 Victors condemned by Armourer	
	June 3	3	Went to Rennighelst. Went to BOO abt Lewis gun tripods. At home my Sec.	
	June 4	4	Sent new Armrs a day or two left in Armoury by rail	
	June 5	5	Went to Brielen and to 2nd Army Gun Park. Unable to get any tripods except from same	
	June 6	6	Fetched Lewis gun from Gun Pk. Barrels badly worn, unserviceable, no use to get a whole gun tested — a typical example of the Army. Let a while in men they kay a part	
	June 7	7	Div" had Sanitäters to 2nd Army attack. Losses of min? v material relatively light. ACOS called	
	June 9	9	Sent to Lewis & M gun to replace one beginning but nothing comparable into the Somme last year	
	June 10	10	Went to Ordnce Workshops at Hoogh & Brielen or receipt of wires from Gun Pk to ask for Armoury to supply (which are getting entirely too) Him to ACOS abt it the went back this last from Workshops. No success. Went to 8 Corps EM Shop or afternoon again fruitlessly. to will constitute number of RO spare Se me of CIOM 2nd Army went into matters lack a view to standardising Gun Park supply.	
			18pdr arrived in the Evening	
	June	11	Lt WATERS A1A arrived to inspect Divl Armourers Shop & Armouries in the Battns	
	June	12	ACOS called Staff Meeting. Lt WATERS went back to BASOS 47 Div"	
	June	14	General Gossip MG & Mortars have come in. The letters are to be taken by 2nd Army TM School	
	June	16	BASOS 38 Bn called. Maxr trophies being received every day.	
	June	18	ACOS called	
	June	19	ACOS called RA sent to return 6 Heavy Mortars — which I certainly dont want here	
	June	21	ACOS ACOS & USA representative called to inspect Workshop	
	June	22	HQ moved to WESTOUTRE French Verifier did not come, as expected, to day	
	June	23	ACOS called Order to move up hell or a/c of shelling, but troop will have to stop here	

Army Form C. 2118.

WAR DIARY
or
INTELLIGENCE SUMMARY
(Erase heading not required.)

BADOS 41 Div." Sheet 2 (June 1917)

Place	Date	Hour	Summary of Events and Information	Remarks and references to Appendices
RENINGHELST	1917			
	June 25		Div" will move into rest at end part of week. Demands for clothing very heavy. Men seem loth to return from leave when especially S.D.	
	June 27		Went to DHQ at WESTOUTRE & to BRANDHOEK to see 23rd Div" Dump which I shall take over	
	June 28		Packing up stores preparing to move	
	June 29.		Stores being sent over to new Dump. Eg gas helmets & armourers shop to day	
	June 30		Got a lot of things to BRANDHOEK. 23rd Div" Ordnance will probably take over this dump here.	

J Stranger Capt.
DADOS 41 Div"

30/vi/1917
DADOS 41 Div"

Army Form C. 2118.

WAR DIARY
or
INTELLIGENCE SUMMARY

July 1917 DADOS 1st Div.

No. 15

Place	Date	Hour	Summary of Events and Information	Remarks and references to Appendices
BERTHEN	July 1		Moved by M.T. lorry. On arr. about 2 mls from village t.D.M.O. Office & stn in tents	
	July 3		Road to bad use. Am going to try issuing dixies for lorries at the same time as lorries draw rations & at same place	
			Went to Corps Hqrs then DADOS	
	July 4		CAESTRE to railhead. Let store field to army to day	
	July 5		Yesterday, stay camp & has issued on new plan as far as possible	
	July 9		GSO issued	
	July 10		Wrote letter Roll Partly Sun 2 or 3 AJJA Bdes to attempts to additionally	
		11	Proceeded on leave Col Trimmer took duty too	
		11	A.P.A. would write to activg DADOS 31st Division to	
		21	receive orders to report to 33rd Division too.	
		23	Orders to move to Westoutre then 33rd River Thanet to Hazebrouck Hazebrouck Home for 123 Bde	
		25	Arrive camp once Ypres to Westoutre - raining	
		28	Then to Croisil to Belvoir Secondary Bays It got Funds Covered Westcott position	
			On Bijart 122 + 123.	
		29	Arrived to Romarin Darm. Castre It got drill cutter SA regularly serviced by	
			123 Bijart. 3rd Canadians Divn at Bus Transport	

31 JUL 1917
D.A.D.O.S
1st DIVISION

G Stevenson Captain
a/DADOS

Army Form C. 2118.

Sheet 1

WAR DIARY
or
INTELLIGENCE SUMMARY.
(Erase heading not required.)

BASOS. 41st Div.   August 1917.   Vol 16

Place	Date 1917	Hour	Summary of Events and Information	Remarks and references to Appendices
Westoutre	Aug 1		Received phone message from Staff Capt 122 Brigade that 81 200 suits for limelights arrived as others units similarly short — I ordered for 600 suits by train.	
	2		Secured the invoice for clothing by 900 suits and Rm Total 1500.	
	7		Had a quiet today from Colonel DDOS 2nd Army who had a look over the Stores. Returned from leave this morning.	
	13		The Division less the R.A. will move to rest to morrow. The R.A. are to be transferred to the 39th Div. We let our PCO take this.	
Berthen	14		Moved to day. Saw bus of 39th Div. & 41st D.A, arranged to supply our R.A units by Sending lorry to La Clytte.	
	15		Div Armours Res SMM DDPG & Caps & ADOS called. Went to HD HQ 3rd & to B Queens also 198 FA. Our heavy W.O. (Ratley) Bae gone to Werrens te enquire & the R.A Armourers & 39th Div will have to entrain there.	
	16			
	17		Lawson (Joseph) v lorry.	
	20		Moved here to day. Location Sheet 36 b N.E 72 C 5 b. Stores will have to go into tents at back of office. Consult he to-morrow ruling of QMS Berry Friday, & let troops should draw less & rest with this latter.	
Wizernes	21			
	22		QM Colpman this morning. My to Bde H.Qrs till room into tents can be made & 3 Coys of ty Bd RDA.	
	24		Saw Col yet armed Sert he moved here. L/Cpl Colter arrived in replacement of K/Corp Scoat Club Carbon	
	25		Still no stew - Had unclassified men reduced to stores & first rent is to number of Bor A to X Coys.	
	26			
	27		Went to St Omer [?] to enquiry. Still to Stores Caps very flaps & pyter to inquire to get the limelight hats you Qasrei Rifle trigger clips [?] & to stores, as to what [?] we have been been issued for Caps, & telephoned Stores No.4	

Army Form C. 2118.

BASRA (Sul 2)
4¹ Div
August 1917

WAR DIARY
or
INTELLIGENCE SUMMARY.
(Erase heading not required.)

Instructions regarding War Diaries and Intelligence Summaries are contained in F. S. Regs., Part II. and the Staff Manual respectively. Title pages will be prepared in manuscript.

Place	Date	Hour	Summary of Events and Information	Remarks and references to Appendices
MARDAN	Aug 30		No stores yet. Apparently Rly has gone to BUKKUR as Q suggested to Corps last week.	
	Aug 31		Q.M. ruling. Non arrival of stores has put him in quandary as to what to demand on bulk indents	J. Spearys Capt BASOS 4¹ Div

Army Form C. 2118.

DADOS / 41st
SEPTEMBER 1917
Vol 17

WAR DIARY Sheet 1.
or
INTELLIGENCE SUMMARY
(Erase heading not required.)

Instructions regarding War Diaries and Intelligence Summaries are contained in F. S. Regs., Part II. and the Staff Manual respectively. Title pages will be prepared in manuscript.

Place	Date	Hour	Summary of Events and Information	Remarks and references to Appendices
	1917			
WIZERNES	Sept 2		Stores largely sent to BRUARAH during last 10 days arrived. Not issued (as usual now) does not facilitate matters, but luckily it	
	Sept 3		Cased to rain after midday. Units have come in well to draw and a wet day has been a relief to help R.S.O. BRUARAH who did not recognised its important. Sent off four Box on Thursday back to CALAIS. Heaven only knows why. However this is now the only truck left, matters forced CALAIS to return it.	
	Sept 6		O.C. Sent urgent issue to CALAIS for Compasses. I took a rest this night to myself.	
	Sept 7		Q.M. meeting. Base wired that no Compasses are obtainable. "Stock nil"!	
	Sept 9		BASOS 7th Div. Which half succeed us on this area come to day. Move will be about 14"	
	Sept 12		Cary-Carroll has obtained some old dump at RENINGHELST which will be only about 4 miles for DHQ.	
	Sept 13		Orders sent to advance tech Stores to RENINGHELST yesterday forward 23rd Div Order 1st Position Div. So was unable to shift anything for two having some 2nd lay forward SAAG to suggest to and after they to went to new one to day	
	Sept 15		X Corps Camp Hill Wady Monday let 23rd Div stuff until is for left the dump. About 11 p.m. they cancelled the V moved us to 24 Div Order dump. (about 23rd had son of Unfortunately traded.)	
2nd RENINGHELST	Sept 15		Moved to 24 Div dump. Hard walking here — it & also especially not so our area or X Corps area taken — lets taken by rather young. The told they have been a typical example of the business like methods of organization that prevails in Corps. Individuals likely we are paying 7–8 notices a day.	
	Sept 16		Lewis – one of Corce bell does, looking had to collect from CARSSAF to special stores for issue for operations. Our	
			Carroll took inquiry me to trace this side. Was I sent on to Q to dent with	

Army Form C. 2118.

BADOS WAR DIARY Sheet 2
41 "DIV" INTELLIGENCE SUMMARY SEPTEMBER 1917
(Erase heading not required.)

Place	Date	Hour	Summary of Events and Information	Remarks and references to Appendices
	1917			
LEVECKEN	Sept 17		On getting in large consign of special stores - Packsaddles Cradles, Armour Coverlets, Yukon packs, horse Collars, Water Carts Pkg. stores &c	
			Kent Cottage. Issued horse picketed Units demanding Gas apparatus, which shews clearly as they must have discarded on the march or not	
			taken the limit to Camp positions	
	Sept 19		Got a Divine Gun Group M.G. stores looking an army of a nature of an being destroyed. New railhead system for Ordn only at OOSTROOSEN	
			A Sectn. left having 5 or 6 lines left. Selroy being declared a dangerous for unloading	
	Sept 21		ADOS called. Saw 1.0.M as to moving at Sprengs Battle of yesterday still in progress	
	Sept 22		Div. (less AR A.E Pioneers No.1 Cy. Train) will move to OOSTRE to-morrow.	
OOSTRE	Sept 23		Moved to-day, but had to leave some men behind as "little stuff" eg Extra pad saddles. Crates &c had to be brought in by	
			Units to LEVECKEN and sent by me to 66 X Corps Troops. This is a big undertaking, under the circumstances, both horses	
			engaged in moving to this place. Realized to be closed stores brought here, Units to be picked & filled, office got going, & stores	
			issued to troops to-morrow.	
	Sept 25		Stores moving little stuff from LEVECKEN to X Corps Troops	
	Sept 26		Moved to LA PANNE. Sheet 11 W.20 b.10.10.	
LA PANNE	Sept 28		Demand for Lost Lewis & Vickers Guns coming in. 123 M.G Coy lost return 20 & 30"	
	Sept 30		Gallery Handcarts at to Troops from 66 XV Corps Troops. Stores came up to ADINKERKE - OOSTHOEK	

11/x/1917

J. Spragge Cpt.
DADOS 41 Div'

COPY.

WAR DIARY
& INTELLIGENCE SUMMARY.
(Erase heading not required.)

Army Form C. 2118.
October 1917.
(Sheet 1.)

Place	Date 1917	Hour	Summary of Events and Information	Remarks and references to Appendices
	Oct.			
LA PANNE	1		Indents for m.g.s still coming in. 238 M.G.Coy. left, completing estabmt. by taking guns from 122 & 124 M.G. Coys.	
	2		Went to Corps H.Q. & saw A.D.O.S. Nearly all first blankets now issued.	
	5		A.D.O.S. called. All Lewis & Vickers guns now received, but some spares still wanted on wired indents for guns.	
ST. IDESBALDE	7		Moved to ST. IDESBALDE, charging places with 42nd Divn. Stores in tent (which blew down) left by 42nd Divn.	
	8		Gale of wind continues. Tents in this condition are hopeless. Cdr. Davison got part of R.E. store & so saved situation. 41st D.A. "moved" back to me for supply.	
	10		Sent blankets out to D.A. at GHYVELDE & PETITE SYNTHE. They suddenly awaken to lack of equipment.	
	11		S/C. Richardson went to 187 & 190 Bdes. & Btys. It seems that 187 Bde. has completed itself for the time being by denuding 190. Result will be probably chaos as regards stores. A.D.O.S. called & went into question of R.A. deficiencies.	
	12		Q.M. meeting.	
	13		Divl. Conference. Am reviewing old indents & cancelling a lot.	

Army Form C. 2118.

COPY.

WAR DIARY
or
INTELLIGENCE SUMMARY.
(Erase heading not required.)

(Sheet 11.)

October 1917.

Instructions regarding War Diaries and Intelligence Summaries are contained in F. S. Regs., Part II. and the Staff Manual respectively. Title pages will be prepared in manuscript.

Place	Date 1917	Hour	Summary of Events and Information	Remarks and references to Appendices
	October.			
	16		Saw Staff Captain R.A. & got out list of R.A. requirements as to guns & howitzers. 9 guns due from IX Corps & 1 How. from X Corps.	
	18		The 1st D.A. attached moving out today. Went to H.Q. 123 Inf. Bde.	
	19		Q.M. meeting. Second blanket being issued, drawn from XV C.T. 3000 Jerkins arrived.	
	20		Divl. Conference.	
	24		Violent storm in night blew down marquee through pole breaking.	
	25		Q.M. meeting today instead of Friday.	
	26		Away all day at G.C.M. at LA PANNE.	
	28		Orders arrived to move whole Divn. at once, fully equipped.	
MALO Les BAINS	29		Moved to MALO LES BAINS. Went to CALAIS & back with S/C. Brownie to arrange about expediting stores. Special arrangements will be made to give us priority.	
	30		Lorries removed to go by road to next destination. Of 2 trucks advised only 1 arrived & that at wrong railhead (St. IDESBALDE & not LEFFERINKHOUCKE). Saw S.M.T.C. XV Corps who arranged to send 4 lorries to pick up stores at St. IDESBALDE, which R.T.O. had kindly promised to load up.	
	31		A large mass of stores, including Jerkins, drawers, socks, came up. Went to D.D.C.S. 4th Army in morning & to O.O. XV C.T. in afternoon. Sent down very large demands today as well as last night by special D.R.L.s to CALAIS.	

sd/ F.J. SPRANGER, Capt.,
D.A.D.O.S. 41st Division.

31/X/1917.

www.ingramcontent.com/pod-product-compliance
Lightning Source LLC
Chambersburg PA
CBHW081249170426
43191CB00037B/2097